WHEELS!

MOIRA BUTTERFIELD

FRANKLIN WATTS
LONDON • SYDNEY

Weird True Facts!... the boring stuff...

This edition published 2014 by Franklin Watts

Copyright © Franklin Watts 2014
Franklin Watts
338 Euston Road
London NW1 3BH

Franklin Watts Australia
Level 17/207 Kent Street
Sydney, NSW 2000
All rights reserved.

A CIP catalogue record for this book
is available from the British Library.

Dewey no: 621.8'2

ISBN: 978 1 4451 2972 3

Printed in China.

Franklin Watts is a division of Hachette Children's Books,
an Hachette UK company
www.hachette.co.uk

Series editor: Sarah Ridley
Editor in chief: John C. Miles
Designer: www.rawshock.co.uk/Jason Anscomb
Art director: Jonathan Hair
Picture research: Diana Morris

Picture credits: AF Archive/Alamy: 7b. Bettmann/Corbis: 12b. bibircha/Shutterstock: 17b. Bibliotheque des Arts Decoratifs Paris/Dagli Orti/Art Archive: 7t. Mary Louise Blanchet, 1903: 17t. Steve Blogg/Rex Features: 23b. Intelligent Bike by Chris Boardman: 25t. Horace Bristol/Corbis: 11b. John Chapple/Getty Images: 26b. Mirror Image by Dennis Clay, photo © Harrod Blank, www.artcaragency.com: 29t. Corbis: 9t.Carl Court/PA Archive/PAI: 27t. Neal Cousland/Shutterstock: 26t. EON Productions/MGM:22b. Everett Collection/Rex Features: 27c. Frederic Le Floc/Rex Features: 20. FWA: 11t, 16. risteski goce/Shutterstock: 18b. Cat Car created by Marian Goodell & Tom Kennedy, photo © Harrod Blank, www.artcaragency.com: 28. The Grainger Collection/Topfoto: 14t. Hulton-Deutsch/Corbis: 13t. Rolf Kosecki /Corbis: 19c. Reinhard Krause/Reuters: 13b. Vladimir Meinik/Shutterstock: 19t. National Motor Museum/HIP/Topfoto: 17c. Peugeot: 24t. plamens art/Shutterstock: 18t. Poodles Rock/Corbis: 12t. PARKcycle designed and fabricated by Rebar in collaboration with Reuben Margolin. Photo Rebar/Andrea Scher: 29b. Rex Features: 24t. Sipa Press/Rex Features: 19b, 21t, 21c. Slavolijub Pantchi/Shutterstock: 8bl inset. Kristina Stasiuliene/Shutterstock: front cover cr, 10t. Cory Thoman/Shutterstock: 6br. Irina Tischenko/Shutterstock: 10b. Topfoto: 14b. Martial Trezzini/epa/Corbis: front cover br, 23t. Ullsteinbild/Topfoto: front cover bl, 15t. Unimedia South America/Rex Features: 29c. Duncan Walker/istockphoto: 15b. Mark Wallace Wikimedia Commons CC some rights reserved: 22t. Warner Bros/DC Comics/Kobal Collection: 27b. Jim Watts/Rex Features: 9b. © Ben Wilson Design www.benwilsondesign.co.uk: front cover cl, 25b. Zuzule/Shutterstock: 8bl.

Every attempt has been made to clear copyright. Should there be any inadvertent omission please apply to the publisher for rectification.

CONTENTS

BEGINNINGS

Without wheels we wouldn't have any way to power the transport and machinery we have today. Luckily for us some unknown genius once had a brilliant idea…

TURNING TIMELINE

4500 BCE
The first known wheels were used in Mesopotamia (modern-day Iraq) and Central Europe. They were solid discs of wood.

2000–1200 BCE
The Hittite People of the Middle East were the first to use a wheel axle, making their chariots lighter and more stable. They became brilliant chariot-drivers.

2200–1550 BCE
Wheel spokes and chariots were invented. The oldest chariots ever found were made by the Andronova People in the Urals (Russia), in 2000 BCE. They buried chariots with their dead.

1325 BCE
Ancient Egyptian boy-emperor Tutankhamun was buried with four hunting chariots. He may have died after breaking a leg, perhaps falling off a chariot.

PASS THAT LOG

Thousands of years ago, if people wanted to move something heavy they put logs underneath and rolled it along, but had to keep replacing the logs at the front as they moved forward. At last someone brainy thought of fixing the logs to make axles and adding wheels, but nobody knows exactly when it happened.

Chariot-racing shown on an ancient Greek vase.

680 BCE

The ancient Greeks made chariot-racing an event at the early Olympic Games.

467–458 BCE

The Persians fitted their war chariots with scythes – long sharp knives sticking out of the wheels. Their Greek enemies soon learnt to move out of the way.

1275 BCE

The Battle of Kadesh, the first recorded chariot battle, between the Hittites and the ancient Egyptians. The Egyptians drew hieroglyphs saying they won, but historians think it was a draw.

530 BCE

The date of the Monteleone chariot – the best-preserved ancient chariot in the world. It was dug up by a farmer in Italy. The skeletons of two people were sitting in it.

COME ON, YOU BLUES!

Chariot-racing was popular in ancient Rome. There were four teams – the greens (prasini), reds (russata), whites (alba) and blues (veneti). The race track had tight corners, and chariot wheels often broke with the strain of turning, which added to the excitement.

Roman chariot-racing reconstructed in the Hollywood movie *Ben Hur*.

YOUR CARRIAGE AWAITS

BUMPY RIDES

Over the centuries different kinds of horse-drawn carriages developed. Many gave their passengers a bumpy dangerous ride.

For centuries in the Western world it was considered weak for a man to ride in a wheeled vehicle. This changed in the 1500s, when nobles started using carriages.

Early carriages didn't have brakes. To stop them, the driver had to pull on chains looped around the wheels.

Suspension stops vehicles bumping and swaying, but wasn't invented until the 1600s. Riding in a carriage before that time would have been a very uncomfortable jerky ride.

Nobles had grand carriages with servants standing on the back and a footman running ahead to clear the way. The more horses you had pulling the carriage, the wealthier you looked.

Glass windows were fitted in carriages from the late 1600s, but English noblewoman Lady Peterborough forgot and accidentally stuck her head through her new glass.

ALL ABOARD

Stagecoaches travelled from town to town in the 1700s to 1800s, like modern bus services. The rich bought seats inside, but the poor sat on the back or on the roof amongst the luggage. If the weather was bad they just had to pull their cloaks over their heads.

Stagecoach companies often employed coach dogs – Dalmatians – to trot alongside their carriages. They looked smart, got along well with horses, killed rats in the stables at night and could run for miles without tiring.

Bling on wheels

Britain's gold State Coach was built in 1762. It is covered in gold leaf, and is reputedly insured for £50 million. It is used for important Royal events, but it gives a bumpy ride and is nicknamed 'old rattlebones'.

The State Coach is covered with decoration and is very heavy.

How to make a carriage wheel

What you need:

- Years of training to be a wheelwright (wheel maker).

- Different types of wood gathered at different times of year and then left to 'season' for five or six years.

- Lots of woodworking tools, some iron and a friendly blacksmith.

What you do:

1. Carve a nave (hub) from strong elm wood. Get a blacksmith to fit iron bands round it.

2. Make oak spokes and hammer them into your nave. Then fit on wooden felloes (wheel sections).

3. Ask the blacksmith to 'shoe' your wheel by fitting an iron rim around it.

4. Hollow out your nave and fit it with an iron box to take the end of the axle.

In seventeenth century London wheelwrights could be fined for making "rotten wheeles".

**Wheelwrights finishing off a wheel.
The centre part is the nave.**

iron rim

nave (hub)

spoke

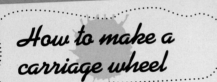

FEET + WHEELS

As well as being used for transport, wheels turned out to be a great way of driving machinery. Their turning power helped to power the Industrial Revolution.

A treadmill, the kind that hamsters run on (left), is a type of wheel. Attached to an axle, it can power things – winding a bucket from a well, for instance. Roman prisoners were sometimes made to walk inside treadmills to lift water from lead mines, and were forced to keep working until they dropped dead.

Dogs, sheep and horses have been used to power treadmills connected to machinery, especially on farms in the 1800s.

In 2005, UK schoolboy Peter Ash invented a hamster-powered mobile phone charger. He attached his hamster's wheel (left) to a generator that powered the charger.

SMALL WHEEL, BIG POWER

Picture the cogs of a small wheel slotted into the cogs of a larger wheel (left). When the small wheel moves, the larger wheel moves, too – but with greater power, because it is bigger. That makes the wheel a 'torque multiplier'. Torque is the name for the twisting force that turns something round. Cogged wheels, called gears, pass on torque.

Gears help power all kinds of modern machinery, but one of the first people to use them was Greek inventor Archimedes (287-212 BCE), when he created giant catapults to use against his enemies the Romans.

Wind + wheels

Wind has been used to turn wheels since at least the first century BCE, when Hero of Alexandria invented a musical organ powered by a wind wheel. This genius created other great ideas, such as a water organ, a coin slot-machine and talking statues.

Old-fashioned windmills and modern wind turbines work using wind to turn their blades, passing on the power via gears inside them.

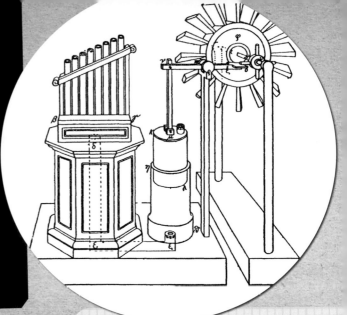

A drawing of Hero's wind-powered musical organ.

A Japanese woman powers a bamboo treadmill to drain a farmer's field in the 1950s.

WATER + WHEELS

Giant waterwheels once powered flour mills. They were turned by running water and connected to gears in the mill buildings that drove the flour-grinding equipment. Human-powered treadmill wheels are still used in some parts of the world to operate pumps, draining fields for agriculture.

GO WEST!

In the 1800s wheels helped to open up the world. People began to travel a lot more, thanks to the development of better wheeled transport.

In the mid-1800s thousands of people travelled westwards across the USA in search of a new life. They piled their possessions into covered wagons called prairie schooners. The wagons had no suspension, so they were a very rough ride and most people did the journey walking or riding alongside them.

You can still see wagon wheel ruts made by the prairie schooners on some of the old trails stretching across America.

Prairie schooners were pulled by oxen, stronger and with more staying power than horses.

Wheels and water

The giant paddle wheels of paddle steamers were turned by steam power, made by burning coal or wood. In the 1800s these ships carried passengers and cargo up the giant rivers of the USA and Australia, powered by wood cut from the riverbanks.

The first Atlantic crossing by a paddle steamer was a race between the British *Great Western* and a small Irish steamer called the *Sirius*, in 1838. The crew of the *Sirius* ran out of coal and burnt their cabin furniture and a mast to keep going. They beat the *Great Western* by a day.

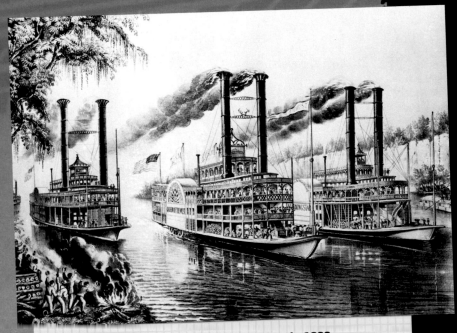
Steamboats race up the Mississippi River in 1866.

A reconstruction of the first ever passenger railway, between Stockton and Darlington, UK.

People power

In Asia, wheelpower has often been human. For centuries the Chinese pushed cargo across their country using the wheelbarrow. It was probably invented by the Chinese army around 200 CE, and it was kept a military secret for many years. Chinese sailing wheelbarrows were fitted with a mast and a sail to help them move along.

Rickshaws are small passenger wagons pulled by a human. Chinese inventor Wu Yulu has built a battery-powered robot, called Wu 25, to pull his rickshaw. He takes it on daily shopping trips to his local village.

TRAIN WHEELS TURN

Wagons and steamboats soon gave way to steam trains, with wheels fitted into rails. The first steam-hauled passenger train ran in the UK in 1825. The passengers mainly sat in open coal wagons, and must have been spattered with steamy smut from the engine. Many people were afraid to travel in the new trains because they thought they might die if they moved at speed.

Wu Yulu and his battery-powered rickshaw robot.

HOT WHEELS

Nicholas Cugnot's wagon, powered by a giant steam boiler.

Before cars and modern-style bicycles were developed, there were all kinds of unusual wheeled vehicle inventions, some of them very dangerous-looking. Would you dare to try any of these?

HOT...OR NOT

The first steam-powered vehicle was built in 1770 by French military engineer Nicholas Cugnot. When he tested it out in Paris, bystanders were very scared, especially when he crashed it into a wall. It had a giant hissing steam boiler that powered the wagon very slowly and ran out of steam every ten minutes.

Steam basics

Steam engines power vehicles by burning fuel to heat water in a boiler, to make steam. The steam expands, pushing pistons that turn a crankshaft attached to wheels.

In 1803 British engineer Robert Trevithick fitted a stagecoach on top of a big steam boiler. His first attempt sank into the road and his second burnt up. His third one was a success, and steam-powered coaches ran regularly around Britain until railways became popular.

A British steam carriage of the early 1830s.

BONE-SHAKING BICYCLES

It's a wonder bicycles ever caught on. The first ones were very uncomfortable and dangerous. The first ever bicycle was the 'dandy horse'. It had no pedals or engine, and was simply powered by running along the road. The dandy horse was briefly fashionable in London in 1819, and caused chaos on pavements.

The Michaux, nicknamed the 'boneshaker', was invented in France in the 1860s, and it started the first big cycling craze. It got its name because its iron-shod wooden wheels gave a very bumpy ride.

In 1870 the penny farthing bicycle, with a giant front wheel, became fashionable. It had comfortable rubber tyres and lightweight spokes, but cyclists who went over bumps ran the risk of going over the handbars. It was common for penny farthing cyclists to get broken bones.

By 1890 the 'safety bicycle' had replaced the penny farthing. It was much safer, easier to ride, more comfortable and faster. Everybody wanted one!

In 1805 US inventor Oliver Evans created America's first steam-powered road vehicle, the 'Oruktor Amphibolos'. It was really a boat on wheels, with a steam engine to drive it down to the river for launching.

Not everyone was happy with steam-powered road vehicles. People complained that they were dangerous, noisy and scared horses. In 1834 sabotage was suspected when a Scottish steam-powered carriage blew up, killing four passengers.

Brave cyclists risk breaking their bones to try the penny farthing.

ON THE ROAD

In 1886 the era of the car began when German engineer Karl Benz invented a petrol-driven 'tricycle'. It was the first true car, and it led to others being developed.

Bertha's big ride

Karl Benz didn't think his invention would be very popular, but his wife Bertha decided to prove him wrong. In 1888 she and her two teenage sons crept out of the house while he was asleep. They sneaked the new car out of the garage and took it on the first ever long-distance drive, a trip of 106 km.

There were no petrol stations or garages, so when they had mechanical problems they got help from a blacksmith, a shoemaker and a farmer on the way. Bertha also used one of her hairpins and a stocking garter to do running repairs.

They got water for the engine from village wells and puddles, and they bought petroleum spirit from a local chemist. In those days you could only buy small bottles of it, for getting stains off clothes.

When they reached their destination, a local town, they sent a telegram to Karl to tell him where they were, and they drove back three days later. Their trip got lots of publicity for the new invention.

Karl Benz (on right) in the world's first car

First across America

In 1903 Horatio Nelson Jackson, a US doctor, won a bet of $50 that he could become the first person to drive one of the newfangled cars across America. It didn't bother him that he had no car, no maps, and hadn't learnt to drive.

He bought a second-hand 'Winton' car and took along a mechanic called Sewall Crocker on the trip, from west to east across the States.

On the way he bought a dog called 'Bud', who did the journey in driving goggles.

During the journey all sorts of things fell out of the car and were lost as it bumped along, including Jackson's glasses and his coat containing all his money. The two men had to repair the car, haul it through streams, and get help from friendly locals on their 63-day trip to New York.

Car production really took off in the USA in 1908, when Henry Ford began making the Model T Ford, much cheaper than any other car on the market at the time.

DANGEROUS DAYS

The first cars had no roof or safety belts, and it was easy to fall out. They operated on one single speed and had to be wound up with a crank at the front of the car. The crank could easily spin backwards and break someone's fingers. Breakdowns were frequent, fuel was difficult to get and roads were very rough in the early days, but by 1900 mass car production had begun in the USA and France.

Early cars looked like carriages, were open to the elements and broke down frequently.

BRILLIANT BASICS

Modern cars have around 15,000 working parts, but still work by the basic principles of early cars.

Inside an internal combustion engine, fuel and air are ignited (burnt) using an electric spark. The burning creates gases that expand in the engine and push pistons.

The in and out motion of the pistons is converted by the engine crankshaft into a turning motion.

The crankshaft powers the driveshaft which turns the wheels. A gearbox alters the power going to the driveshaft to make the car go slower or faster.

spark plug

piston

crankshaft

TREAD CAREFULLY

Take a look at some of these true tyre facts for a new angle on the world of wheels.

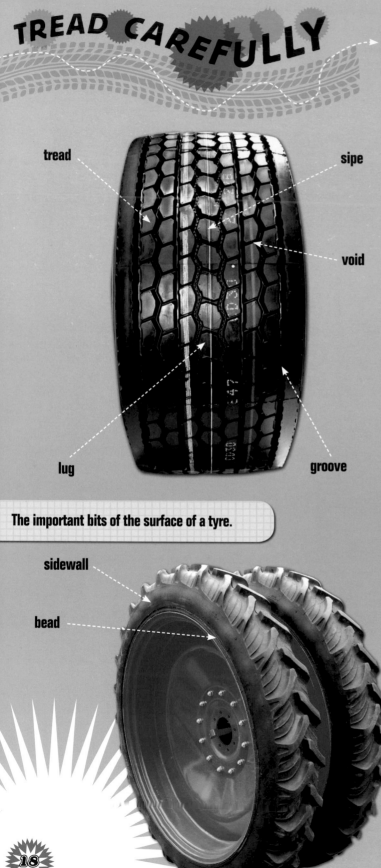

tread

sipe

void

lug

groove

The important bits of the surface of a tyre.

sidewall

bead

Tread carefully

Tread gives tyres traction – grip on the road. Different tyres have different tread patterns depending on what kind of road they are likely to be driven on.

Bead The part of the tyre which connects to the wheel rim. It is reinforced with wire.

Sidewalls The sides of the tyre, reinforced inside with metal cord or fabric.

Tread The part of the wheel that comes in contact with the road surface.

Lugs The raised part of the tread in contact with the road.

Grooves Channels that run round the tyre, to help to drain water away.

Voids Spaces between the lugs.

Sipes The pattern cut across the tread.

Old tyres are shredded and made into carpet underlay and carpet tiles.

Every year toy company Lego make around 330 million mini tyres for their toy vehicles.

BIGGEST

The world's biggest tyres are found on the Le Tourneau L-2350 mining loader. They have a diameter of 4m (13ft), a width of 1.78m (5.83ft), and cost around $62,500 each.

Giant truck tyres are far too heavy for a person to carry. They can weigh over 50 tonnes.

Mud and snow tyres are designed with tread patterns to help them grip on to uneven or slippery surfaces.

SPIKIEST

Ice-speedway is a popular sport in Russia, Sweden and Finland. The speedway bikers race over ice tracks using tyres fitted with 3cm metal spikes, to get a grip on the frozen surface.

Around one billion vehicle tyres are manufactured every year around the world.

Most bling

The world's most expensive wheels cost $1 million dollars for four. Made by US company Asanti, the wheel rims are encrusted with diamonds and rubies. The company gives away a free car with each set of wheels.

$ 1.000.000

4 Icelink Rims
$1.000.000
included Bentley Coupe
& 1 year Bodyguard 24/7

WINNING WHEELS

SECRETS OF SUCCESS

To be a winner in any wheeled sport, you need to get the very best performance from your machinery.

An expert Formula One crew can change all four wheels in around 3.5 seconds.

Brilliant basics

Most cars have two-wheel drive, which means only two of the wheels – either the front or the back ones – get power from the engine.

Four-wheel drive cars provide engine power to all four wheels, which gives the vehicle better grip and control on bumpy uneven surfaces such as off-road tracks.

WINNING WHEEL SECRETS

Formula 1 teams choose between different types of tyres, depending on the track conditions and the weather. Putting on the wrong tyres could cost the race or even cause an accident. Cars may have to change tyres during the course of a race, and it must be done as quickly as possible. Formula One pit crews use air guns to quickly undo wheel nuts and then fit on replacement wheels with pre-heated tyres. It takes an expert crew about 3.5 seconds to change all four wheels.

The Dakar Rally is probably the toughest test of car tyres in the world.

Tour de France cyclists have very thin tyres that cut through the air.

World's toughest races

The Dakar Rally is the world's toughest long-distance driving race. Cars, motorbikes and trucks can enter the gruelling challenge, which takes place over 16 days across 9,000km of rough dangerous terrain. Originally run in Africa, the race currently takes place across South America, and its drivers must cross the Andes Mountains and the barren Atacama Desert. Usually only about half the competitors make it to the end.

One of the toughest bicycle races in the world is the RAAM (Race Across AMerica), which crosses the USA from west to east. It is run over 22 days, with no breaks or rest days for the riders. Competitors ride on average 539km a day, and their endurance test includes night racing and an overall 30,480m of hill climbing.

The Tour de France is the world's most famous cycle race, and one of the hardest, with 21 stages over a distance of around 3,400km. There are long flat sections, but also steep mountain climbs and fast descents, when the racers must concentrate on speeding round mountain bends at up to 100km/hr. Teams spend thousands on their bikes to get the best results.

SCIENCE ON WHEELS

Concept cars are prototypes made to showcase new technology or style designs. They may look nutty, but have creative elements that might one day get used on everyday vehicles.

SCIENCE ON WHEELS

Relax and watch Internet company Google has tested a driverless car on roads in and around San Francisco, USA. The car has onboard video cameras, radar and laser sensors and uses Google's mapping software to follow a route.

Molecule motor You can't drive the nanocar, built by Rice University, USA, because it is 4 nanometres long and 3 nanometres wide (human hair is about 80,000 nanometres thick). It isn't a real car, but a structure of tiny molecules powered by a solar cell. Nanocars could one day be driven by remote control into someone's body to deliver medicines.

Invisible car An 'invisible car' appeared in the James Bond movie *Die Another Day*, but none has been built for real yet. However, scientists are working on technology called 'optical camouflage', which could be used on warfare vehicles. One method of making a vehicle invisible is to put cameras on an object, film behind it and then project the background scene onto the front of the object.

Google's driverless car being tested in the US.

Piers Brosnan in his 'invisible car' in *Die Another Day*

CARS THAT CARE

The Assystem City Car, a concept car designed in 2007, has lots of innovative ideas. It can detect when a driver is beginning to nod off at the wheel, and has mood settings to change the car's colour and sounds. It also contributes to saving the planet by being 95% recyclable.

Tomorrow's tyres

Sideways driver: The Nissan Torii concept car has spherical ball-shaped wheels that can move freely in any direction, making it much easier to get into tight parking spaces!

Look, no air: Michelin Tweel airless tyres could one day replace tyres filled with air. The spokes and tread are made from plastic material that flexes and changes shape when it goes over a bump, and then springs back again.

Cyber smarts: Cyber tyres have sensors fitted onto them to transmit information such as the tyre's pressure or temperature, alerting the driver to any problems.

CONCEPTS GONE WRONG

Wet idea: In January 1985 the Sinclair C5 electric car was launched. It could travel at 24 km/h but it was a failure because it couldn't go up hills and the driver got wet if it rained. By August 1985 production of the C5 had ceased.

Dangerous drive: In 1958 Ford designed the space-age Ford Nucleon, a car powered by a small nuclear reactor. The Nucleon's powerplant was to work in a similar way to a nuclear submarine, but on a much smaller scale. Luckily for the safety of the world, it was never actually built.

The Sinclair C5, driven by its inventor.

BIKING THE FUTURE

MOTORBIKE MANIA

Designers have used their creativity to come up with cool concept motorbikes and bicycles, too.

Driver lays flat

8.3-litre V10 car engine

four wheels instead of two

horizontal double-fork suspension

Monsterbike Launched in 2003, the Dodge Tomahawk is powered by the enormous V10 car engine usually found in a Dodge Viper supercar. In theory it could go at 480km/h or more, but in reality it isn't stable enough to do really fast speeds and stay upright. Dodge sells these as rideable pieces of modern art.

Not so crazy The BMW *Wahnsinn* is a 2005 concept motorbike. *Wahnsinn* means 'insane' in German, but this sleek-looking design seems very clever. It is powered by a fuel cell, which contains no moving parts and is much less polluting, cheaper and quieter than a standard engine.

Two for one The Peugeot 20Cup is a cross between a motorbike and a car, with one wheel at the back and two at the front. It was launched in 2006 as a race vehicle with its own race series. It has no doors, so the driver has to climb in.

BRAINY BICYCLES

It's true that bicycles work well as they are, but that hasn't stopped designers from trying their best to reinvent the idea.

Spokeless and steal-proof Chris Boardman's solar-powered bike design features puncture-proof tyres, spokeless and chainless wheels and a computer that measures how many calories the rider has used up cycling. It can play music and has a solar-powered engine that kicks in if the rider needs it. It's very hard to steal, too, because it is fitted with a computer locking device that will only open when it recognises the owner's fingerprint.

Future spokes   Find pictures of these amazing concept bicycles online...

The Di-Cycle – A bicycle that works on water as well as on roads.

The Locust Bike – Designer Josef Cadek's take on the fold-down bike, a wacky-looking fun shape that collapses into a neat circle.

The Big Eye Cruiser Bike – A bicycle designed for 10–15-year-olds, that you can extend to make it bigger as you grow.

The sideways bike – A bicycle where the cyclist sits sideways, just for fun.

Monowheel bike – Sit inside this giant wheel (left) and pedal!

Bamboo bikes – With a frame made of lightweight bamboo, specially grown to the right shape.

The cardboard bike – Designed by UK student Phil Bridge, this won't go very fast or far, but it's cheap, easily recycled and apparently rainproof. It probably won't get stolen, either…

XTREME WHEELS

RECORD-BREAKERS

Here is a selection of vehicles that you probably won't see cruising down your street any time soon. They take travelling on wheels to extremes of size and speed!

The world record for the longest roadtrain ever stands at more than 100 trailers.

BIGGEST

The world's largest vehicles are roadtrains – trucks that pull lots of trailers at once. The largest ones, called powertrains, operate in Australia's remote Northern Territory, hauling material from gold mines. They have six trailers and are so heavy they need two engines.

FASTEST

The supersonic World Land Speed record is currently held by Thrust SSC (below) at 1228 kph (763 mph). The Thrust jet car was powered by two fighter jet engines and piloted by fighter pilot Andy Green. It has the power of 145 Formula One cars, or roughly 1,000 family cars.

THRUST SSC

During its record run Thrust broke the sound barrier, causing a sonic boom.

Capable of reaching 1,367.94 kph (850 mph).

Fuel consumption: 18 litres per second (4 Imperial gallons, 4.8 US gallons).

Wheels: aluminium and capable of withstanding huge pressure.

110,000 horsepower

SMALLEST

The smallest street-legal car ever was the Peel P50, first built in 1962. It was just 134.6cm (53in) long and 99.06cm (39in) wide. It had no reverse gear but it did have a handle so the driver could pick up the car and turn it round. The car is so tiny that Jeremy Clarkson was able to drive one through the corridors of the BBC offices, on the show *Top Gear*.

The tiny Peel P50 being driven through London.

James Bond's Lotus Esprit becomes a submarine in *The Spy Who Loved Me*.

Best movie cars

Movie legend James Bond has used lots of super-clever cool cars. His Aston Martin DB5, used in *Goldfinger*, had an ejector seat, machine guns hidden behind the radiator grille and a pop-up shield. In *The Spy Who Loved Me* his Lotus Esprit converted into a submarine.

Probably the coolest movie vehicles of all belong to Batman, the superhero created by DC Comics. He's always adapting his Batmobile, but in the past it has featured a Bat-tering ram, Batphone, all-purpose Bat ray, smoke emitter and nail spreader. According to Batman, the only thing that can penetrate its armour 'isn't from this planet'.

The awesome jet-powered Batmobile, as used in the movies.

STOP PRESS: World speed records are there to be broken! Andy Green hopes to pass 1,000mph (1,609 kph) in the Bloodhound SSC jet car in 2012.

IS IT **A CAR** OR IS IT...

...A PLANE?

The 1922 Leyat had an aeroplane propellor on the front to power it along. In those days everyone thought that cars would eventually fly, but nearly a hundred years later flying cars still haven't taken off.

...A TRAIN?

Japanese engineers have invented a 'dual-mode vehicle', a bus that can drive to a railway station and then turn into a train to run along the rails.

Motoring moggie —This furry feline car could be ideal for cat-loving drivers. It appeared at the Burning Man Festival in Nevada, USA, where lots of cool art cars turn up every year.

Mad masterpieces

'Cartists' are artists who decorate their vehicles, sometimes in ways that are plain crazy. Like this double VW Beetle. But which way is up?

...A SUBMARINE?

The Rinspeed sQuaba is an electric car that can turn into a submarine and dive underwater. The driver has to wear diver's equipment, though.

Do you fancy a picnic, but can't find a green space? You need the Parkcycle, a moveable stretch of greenery that's pedalled round San Francisco, USA.

Axle A bar that connects two wheels together.

Blowout When a tyre punctures and air pressure disappears quickly.

Brakes A device which makes a wheel go slower or stop.

Carriage A horse-drawn passenger vehicle.

Chariot A horse-drawn battle vehicle.

Coach dog Another name for the Dalmatian dog, a breed that was often kept on stagecoaches.

Cog A tooth-like part cut into the edge of a wheel in a machine. The cog can fit between the cogs of another wheel, so that if one wheel turns, the other also turns.

Concept car A futuristic car design that hasn't yet been built commercially.

Crank A turning handle used to start a vintage car engine.

Crankshaft A long metal rod that helps a vehicle engine to turn the wheels. The in and out motion of the engine's pistons is converted by the engine crankshaft into a turning motion.

Cyber tyres Tyres fitted with sensors to record their condition.

Driveshaft A vehicle part that delivers movement created by the power of the engine to the wheels.

Felloes Sections of a wheel, around the outside of the spokes.

Fire box A section of a steam engine where fuel is burnt.

Four-wheel drive When all four wheels of a vehicle receive power from the engine.

Gears Connecting sets of wheels, controlling how much power from an engine goes to the moving parts of a machine.

Gearbox A vehicle part that alters the power going from the engine to the wheels via the driveshaft, to make the vehicle go slower or faster.

Head-up display Where a vehicle's stats – such as speed and fuel consumption – are displayed on the windscreen in front of the driver instead of on dials.

Industrial Revolution A period of time in the early 1800s in western countries, when work began to be done more by machines in factories than by hand at home.

Internal combustion engine An engine where fuel and air are ignited (burnt) using an electric spark. The burning creates gases that expand in the engine and push pistons. The movement of the pistons is transferred to the wheels of a vehicle.

Paddle steamer A boat fitted with giant paddle wheels, driven round by a steam engine.

Paddle wheel A wheel with small flat blades fixed around the edge, which makes a boat move through water or operates a piece of machinery.

Piston A short solid piece of metal which moves up and down inside the cylinder of an engine. The power produced by the pistons is sent to the wheels.

Prairie schooner A type of wagon with a soft cover, used to cross the USA in the 1800s.

Roadtrain A road truck that tows a number of wagons.

Sidewalls The sides of a tyre, reinforced inside with metal cord or fabric.

Spark plug The part of an engine which produces a spark to ignite the fuel.

Spokes Struts radiating out from the centre of a wheel.

Stagecoach A horse-drawn coach for paying passengers, which stopped at different set stages on its journey.

Steam engine An engine where coal is burnt to heat water, creating steam. The pressure of the steam is used to move pistons which power machinery.

Suspension Equipment fixed to the wheels of a vehicle to reduce the bumpiness of the ride.

Torque A force which causes something to turn in a circle.

Traction The ability of a tyre to hold onto the ground without sliding.

Tread The part of a wheel that comes in contact with the road surface.

Treadmill A wheel turned by a human or animal walking inside it.

Two-wheel drive When two wheels of a vehicle receive power from the engine.

Waterwheel A wheel that is designed so that it can be turned by running water.

WEBSITES ON WHEELS

www.mariamilani.com/ancient_rome/Ancient_Roman_Chariot_Races.htm
Interesting description of Roman chariot races.

www.royal.gov.uk/TheRoyalResidences/TheRoyalMews/History.aspx
The British Royal coach collection.

www.sciencemuseum.org.uk
Lots of information and images of wheel-related inventions.

www.stanleymotorcarriage.com
Learn more about steam cars.

www.formula1.com
Lots of information about Formula One cars.

www.weburbanist.com
All sorts of crazy cutting-edge design ideas, including bicycles and cars.

Note to parents and teachers

Every effort has been made by the Publishers to ensure that the websites in this book are suitable for children, that they are of the highest educational value, and that they contain no inappropriate or offensive material. However, because of the nature of the Internet, it is impossible to guarantee that the contents of these sites will not be altered. We strongly advise that Internet access is supervised by a responsible adult.